The [Ju 52]

The Luftwaffe's Workhorse

An aircraft belonging to Wekusta 1/Luftflotte 1 in Russia during 1942 or 1943. Wekusta stands for *Wettererkungdungstaffel* (weather reconnaissance/research unit) and these units collected data on temperature, wind speed, humidity, and air pressure. The writing of names on the sides of the fuselages was common for pre-war civil Ju 52s, but the tradition faded when the war began. This Ju 52, however, still has its name on the fuselage. Note the covered-up electrical generator above the windows.

LUFTWAFFE AT WAR

THE JUNKERS Ju 52
The Luftwaffe's Workhorse

Morten Jessen

Greenhill Books
LONDON

Stackpole Books
PENNSYLVANIA

Greenhill Books

The Junkers Ju 52 first published 2002 by Greenhill Books, Lionel Leventhal Limited, Park House, 1 Russell Gardens, London NW11 9NN
www.greenhillbooks.com
and
Stackpole Books, 5067 Ritter Road, Mechanicsburg, PA 17055, USA

British Library Cataloguing in Publication Data:
Jessen, Morten
The Junkers Ju 52: the Luftwaffe's workhorse –
(Luftwaffe at war; 20)
1. Junkers Ju 52 – History 2. World War, 1939-1945 –
Aerial operations, German
I. Title
940.5'4'4943

ISBN 1-85367-509-1

Library of Congress Cataloging-in-Publication Data available.

Designed by DAG Publications Ltd
Design by David Gibbons
Layout by Anthony A. Evans
Edited by Andy Oppenheimer
Printed in Singapore

Acknowledgements
I would like to thank James Crow for contributing the majority of the photos for this book and for answering my questions. The photos are from his collection unless otherwise noted. I would also like to thank Chris König for material used in the Introduction and captions. Thanks also go to Barry Rosch, Karl Kössler, Peter Petrick and Manfred Griehl who donated photos.

I would also like to thank my friends Michael Dubré and Charles Metz for their advice. Finally, my girlfriend, Dawn Jacob, deserves a mention for her help and patience

LUFTWAFFE AT WAR
THE JUNKERS Ju 52

From the Ju 52/1m to the Ju 52/3m

By the end of 1930 it became obvious that the increase in cargo loads required a new aircraft. *Dipl.-Ing.* Zindel was asked about the possibility of designing a single-engined aircraft capable of transporting 2 tons of payload and with an operational range of 496 miles (800 km). Zindel then redesigned the Junkers W (Ju) 33 and came up with a version made to fit a 1,000-hp engine. For various reasons Junkers could not obtain such an engine, and the first prototype had to be built with a BMW VIIaU engine, developing 750 hp. After a couple of test flights – the first on 13 October 1930 – the aircraft carried a 2-ton payload over a distance of 930 miles (1,500 km), an achievement no other aircraft available could have offered. Canada ordered the first Junkers Ju 52/1m (1m = single engine) immediately. The aircraft was slightly improved by installing an Armstrong-Siddeley 'Leopard' radial engine, developing 800 hp.

The Ju 52/1m featured a freight compartment measuring 20 ft 9 in x 5 ft 4 in x 6 ft 3 in (6.35 x 1.65 x 1.90 m). In order to give easy access to this compartment, Zindel provided three hatches, including a smaller one on top of the fuselage.

Although the very successful earlier designs of Zindel, the Junkers G24 and G31, had been equipped with three engines, the Ju 52/1m proved an excellent platform for a future aircraft. The increase in air traffic and a wish for better safety led to the idea of adding two additional engines to the existing Ju 52/1m construction. This development led to the Ju 52/3m (3m = *Drei Motoren* – three engines).

During the Internationaler Alpenflug (Alpine International Air Show) on 28 June 1932 the Junkers Ju 52/3m was shown to the public for the first time and won first place in the transport plane category.

The civil airliner

After its appearance in the summer of 1932 the Ju 52/3m established a legendary name everywhere, and the *Tante* Ju ('*Auntie* Ju') became known as a comfortable and safe aircraft. By late 1932 the Ju 52/3m was delivered to Deutsche Lufthansa, which tested it on the most heavily travelled routes (Berlin-London and Berlin-Rome). As soon as the Ju 52/3m had proved its potential, Lufthansa expanded its fleet of Ju 52s to more than 230 aircraft.

Other airlines followed soon, and before the outbreak of World War II the Ju 52 saw service in 25 countries worldwide – with more than 30 airlines ordering Zindel's revolutionary design. The Ju 52/3m was sold to many countries, including Argentina, Austria, Belgium, Bolivia, Brazil, Ecuador, Finland, Greece, Hungary, Italy, Peru, Poland, Portugal, Great Britain, South Africa, Spain, Switzerland, Sweden, and Turkey.

Other versions of the Ju 52/3m had changed interiors and various engines according to the company ordering the aircraft. Among these were the BMW 132 A/E and A-3, the Pratt & Whitney 'Hornet' S1eG, the Pratt & Whitney 'Wasp' S3H1-G, Piaggio PXR, Bristol 'Pegasus VI' and Jumo 205 C.

Entering the military service

After Hitler broke the Versailles treaty, the new Luftwaffe looked for a suitable aircraft to equip the Luftwaffe's transport units and decided to order Ju 52s. Therefore the need for a military version of the Ju 52/3m was considered early. The first aircraft built to the specifications of the *Reichswehr* was the Ju 52/3m Sa3, which was used extensively for personnel transport, cargo duties, and pilot training. In 1934 the first truly military version of the Ju 52/3m was put into operation, designated Ju 52/3m g3e and equipped with BMW 132 A-radial engines. The Ju 52 also formed the core of the new bomber units before the He 111, Ju 86 and Do 17 became available in 1936, even though it was not designed to perform in the role as a bomber.

The civil version of the Ju 52 came with a tail wheel, whilst the military version had a tail skid. This tail skid caused problems when manoeuvering the aircraft on airfields. The tail skid was therefore replaced with a tail wheel and this version was designated g4e. By 1939, the Ju 52/3m g4e was the main transport aircraft in service with the Luftwaffe, and most g3e had been rebuilt to this specification.

The Junkers Flugzeug- und Motorenwerke AG had production plants for aircraft in: Dessau, Aschersleben, Bernburg, Halberstadt, Leopoldshall, Leipzig-Mockau and Breslau. Furthermore production was begun at

Letov in Prague by the end of 1938, and at the Paris-Villacoublay plants after the Western campaign. Other companies working for Junkers included Weserflug and ATG.

The Spanish Civil War

When the Spanish Civil War broke out on 18 July 1936, Germany joined sides with the Fascists and sent 20 Ju 52s and six Heinkel He 51s to support them. The Ju 52s were led by *Hauptmann* von Morcau, who had 42 pilots under his command.

The Ju 52s came to play a strategically important role in the course of the war when they transported 8,899 Moorish troops, 44 field guns, 90 heavy machine guns and 137 tons of ammunition from Morocco to Spain in September 1936. When the operation started, each Ju 52/3m carried 22 fully equipped combat troops. Later, the number of troops was increased to 30.

During the Spanish Civil War the Ju 52/3m was also used as a bomber, but by mid-1937 it became evident that this role was unsuitable for the Ju 52/3m. In the late 1930s only horizontal bomb magazines were available, and they could not be installed in the Ju 52 because directly underneath the freight compartment the wing centre section with its four main spars was located. The short distance between the spars did not allow the horizontal positioning of even the small 110-lb (50 kg) bombs. Furthermore, that made the Ju 52 unsuitable in the bomber role was lack of speed and manoeuvrability, making the aircraft easy prey for enemy fighters and anti-aircraft guns. Nevertheless, several Ju 52/3m g4e served in Franco's forces and saw combat with Grupo de Bombardo Nocturno 2-G-22 until 26 March 1939.

Deployment in World War II

The Ju 52/3m were deployed in a variety of roles and on all fronts. The two primary tasks were transportation of personnel and cargo, but in addition it was used to drop paratroopers and tow gliders. The latter roles were the most dangerous because the aircraft had to fly over enemy territory and be exposed to fighters and anti-aircraft guns.

The occupation of Poland went faster than expected and therefore the planned parachute drops were not carried out. The main activity took place in the southern sector where Ju 52s supplied the panzer and motorised units. Losses of Ju 52s in this campaign were light.

During the 6th and 7th of April, 1940, Ju 52s landed at airfields throughout Schleswig-Holstein. Airfields used were Neumünster (KGrzbV 101 and 102), Schleswig (KGrzbV 103), Stade (KGrzbV 104), Kiel-Holtenau (KGrzbV 105), Üterzen (KGrzbV 106), Hamburg-Fühlsbüttel (KGrzbV 107) and Oldenburg. They were to be part of the invasion force that would soon invade Denmark and Norway in operation 'Weserübung'.

Shortly after 7:00 on 9 April, a dozen Ju 52s airlifted paratroopers to capture Aalborg airfield in northern Jutland, which was occupied within hours after the landing. The airfield was needed as a springboard for the invasion of Norway. Even though the invasion of Denmark went on as planned, the capture of Norway turned out to be more difficult than anticipated.

During the first half of the day approximately 900 troops were flown into Fornebu airfield near Oslo, and took the airfield and city. However, the invasion force met more resistance in the Oslo fjord, and this gave the Norwegian royal family and government time to escape to England.

The occupation of Denmark and southern Norway was completed by the end of April; after just ten days the Ju 52s' primary task had been completed and all, except for one *Gruppe*, returned to prepare for the next campaign. The *Transportverbände* lost approximately 150 Ju 52s deployed in Operation 'Weserübung', but the invasion of the lower countries and France would soon make serious inroads into the Luftwaffe *Transportverbände*.

Operation 'Gelb', the invasion of the low countries and France, began on 10 May 1940, and during the early stages made use of 212 Ju 52s under the command of *Generalleutnant* Student. The Luftwaffe lost a significant number of Ju 52s to fighter and anti-aircraft fire during the operation. At Waalhaven airfield many Ju 52s were lost on the ground when Dutch artillery fired at the airfield to slow down the incoming stream of troop carring transports.

On the Eastern Front the *Transportverbände* became especially important because of the vast distances in Russia, and because of the scorched-earth tactics used by the Soviet forces when they retreated. This made the advancing army units more dependent on air supply from the rear when no good or safe roads for trucks were available.

One of the larger German airborne operations during the war was the invasion of Crete, called Operation 'Merkur'. A total of 493 Ju 52/3m and 80 DFS 230 gliders were scheduled to attack in three waves, but problems at the airfields on the Greek mainland made the operation difficult. The few airfields with hard runways were occupied by bomber units of *VIII. Fliegerkorps* and the rest were small and poorly equipped fields of sand. This caused a problem with clouds of dust every time aircraft took off. The sand rose up as high as 3,000 ft (900 m) and seriously limited visibility, which prevented other aircraft from taking off for almost 20 minutes and caused the assembly of a *Gruppe* over the airfields to last more then an hour. The Ju 52s flew low over their target areas and were vulnerable to anti-aircraft fire. The thin metal fuselage and wings gave no protection against gunfire and the result was 151 Ju 52s shot down, including many damaged beyond repair.

When supplying an engaged army group an additional, but important task, appeared – evacuation of wounded soldiers. The biggest operations of this kind were the airlift operations in February 1942 when six German army divisions were trapped at Demjansk, and in November 1942 to February 1943 when the German

Sixth Army was encircled at Stalingrad. During these operations the Luftwaffe lost irreplaceable experienced personnel and the pilot schools were not able to train the replacements, needed to keep the *Transportverbände* at full strength. Nor could the factories produce the number of aircraft lost during these operations.

The Luftwaffe lost 432 transport aircraft, almost all Ju 52/3m, in less then three weeks trying to assist the retreating *Afrikakorps*. The attempts to supply, and later to evacuate, the German troops in Tunisia in April 1943 took a particular severe toll on the *Transportverbände* and marked its future.

Technical developments

The general layout of the Ju 52/3m did not see major alterations during production. However, a huge variety of types and subtypes were constructed, most of which could not be distinguished from the outside. Necessary changes in the radio gear or armament led to new series, while the airframe stayed the same. In addition to the Sa3 and g3e series, the following Ju 52 subtypes were developed:

● The Ju 52/3m g4e was a transport plane with BMW 132 A-engines. The g4e had a reinforced floor and a strengthened undercarriage. To ease the process of loading transport goods, the g4e had a door on top of the fuselage and on the right side of the hull. Weserflug at Bremen-Lemwerder produced the first prototype and a few of the aircraft produced there saw service with Deutsche Lufthansa.
● The Ju 52/3m g5e went into production in 1940 and could alternatively be fitted with wheels or floats. The float version Ju 52/3m g5e (See) was used successfully in deploying mountain troops in Norwegian fjords, which were otherwise inaccessible to paratroops and the army. The g5e was powered by BMW 132T-2 engines, producing 830 hp each, and could be ordered with a 'Schleppsporn 6000' designed to tow gliders.
● The Ju 52/3m g6e was an improved g5e available with ski landing gear to replace the wheels, made with the Russian campaign in mind.
● The Ju 52/3m g7e was a land- or sea-based version powered with BMW 132 T-engines. The size of the right side cargo door was enlarged while the number of the fuselage windows decreased. The instrument panel's layout was modified to accommodate the Siemens-Kurssteuerung K4 (autopilot).
● The Ju 52/3m g8e was basically a g6e without wheel covers, which were found to be a problem on the Eastern Front where mud would build up around the wheel. The g8e also included a 13mm MG 131 in the dorsal position.
● The Ju 52/3m g9e used the airframe and wings of the g6e, but equipped with newer equipment and the BMW 132 Z engine. The g9e was built in small quantities.
● The Ju 52/3m g10e resembled the g7e. An unknown number was built at Weserflug (Bremen), while Amiot in France manufactured approximately 170 aircraft.
● The Ju 52/3m g12e fitted the g7e-/g10e-lines with the BMW 132 Z-engines; only a few aircraft of the g12e-series were produced.
● The Ju 52/3m g14e: during service in Russia many Ju 52/3ms experienced extensive battle damage. Although the airframe often survived attacks, the crews suffered heavy losses. Therefore, Junkers decided to build a bulletproof Ju 52/3m based on the Ju 52/3m g8e, in order to give additional protection to the crews. Only a few of these aircraft saw service.

An unusual modification to the Ju 52/3m was the Ju 52/3m MS – the mine ring version. A common nickname for the MS-version was 'Mausi'. When Dr. Benecke tested a British mine in September 1939, he discovered that a magnetic field could detonate the weapon. A ring, consisting of 44 aluminium rings, diameter 44 ft 9 in–48ft (14-15m), working as a coil and encapsulated in an aluminium casing, was attached to the underside and wings on a Ju 52/3m g4e. Flying at low level above the surface of the North Sea, the Ju 52 blew up several mines near the port of Vlissingen in the Netherlands.

A small number of g4e, g5e, g6e and g7e received the mine ring modifications and as early as 1940 began patrolling the German coasts. When British Wellingtons tried to interrupt traffic on the Danube by laying mines, these Ju 52s cleared the river until the end of the war. Some saw service after the end of World War II when they were attached to the GMSA – German Mine Sweeping Administration (British command).

The Ju 252 and other variants

Construction of the Ju 252 (see page 66) began in 1938, when Deutsche Lufthansa requested improvement on the Ju 52/3m. The original design's designation was EF 77 and had little in common with its predecessor other than having three engines. It featured a hydraulic rear-loading ramp, making loading and unloading of larger equipment easier, and it could transport up to 11 tons of cargo compared to the Ju 52's four-ton capacity. The EF 77 also had a good operational range, making it ideal for covert missions.

The EF 77 was proposed as a replacement for the Ju 52/3m, but its wing design showed some critical aspects and the RLM asked Junkers to re-design it. In early 1940 the RLM ordered three Ju 252s that were assembled in Dessau. The parts were manufactured at factories in Schönebeck and Bernburg. The assembly process of Ju 252 V1 was begun in June 1940 and completed in October 1941. The Ju 252 V1 did, however, not make it's maiden flight until 5 June 1942.

Testing of V1 began on 5 June 1942, but due to political circumstances Lufthansa did not take over the new aircraft. The RLM ordered that the V4 and the following 11 Junkers Ju 252 should be equipped with defensive armament consisting of a MG 131 on the upper fuselage behind the cockpit. The tests, carried out at Rechlin, were not particularly successful and development continued for some time until the weapon pod was ready for operational use.

The V5-V15 aircraft were re-designated as Junkers Ju 252A-1 but kept the serials of prototypes even after the RLM decided not to order further aircraft. Their status as 'V'-flights (*Versuchsmuster* - experimental aircraft) kept them from being assigned to specific units. The military career of these aircraft involved duties delivering Daimler-Benz DB 606-engines for replacement to KG 40's Heinkel He 177 at Bordeaux-Mèrignac, dropping agents in North Africa, and transport of supplies and personnel on all fronts.

Besides the Ju 252, the Junkers Company made two other attempts to produce a follow-up to the Ju 52, designated Ju 290 and Ju 352 – but none reached the same production numbers as the Ju 52. The Junkers Ju 352 would have been the best replacement, but only 46 of these aircraft, called Herkules, saw service.

Organisation of the Luftwaffe transport units

The first transport unit, KGrzbV 1 (*Kampfgruppe zur besondern Vervendung* – Unit for Special Purposes), was formed in October 1937 from IV./KG 152 'Hindenburg', and by the start of the war KGzbV 172, KGrzbV 1, 2, 9 and LLG 1 and 2 had been created (LLG – *Luftlandesgeschwader*, Air Landing Wing). Some of these units were at far from full strength, mainly because the training of pilots and production of aircraft could not keep up with the speed with which the units were created. An example of this problem is shown by I. and II./KGzbV 172, which were formed by using personnel and aircraft from Deutsche Lufthansa. A full-sized *Geschwader* consisted of four *Gruppen,* each with 53 aircraft, (four *Staffeln,* each with 12 aircraft and 5 *Gruppe Stab* aircraft). A KGzbV would therefore total 212 aircraft when in full strength. Many temporary units were formed for major operations such as the invasion of Poland, where KGzbV 'Ahlefeld', made up of several *Gruppen* from existing units and was created specifically for that campaign and then disbanded immediately after in order to return to their original units.

On 1 May 1943 the air transport arm was reorganised with the creation of *XIV. Fliegerkorps.* All transport units in all theatres fell under its command. The backbone of this new command structure was five *Transportgeschwader* (TG 1 to 5). This was done to ensure a strong and unified command structure, but many smaller cargo *Staffeln* were still formed with very specific tasks in mind.

XIV. Fliegerkorps was split up in August 1944 because of losses and the changing war situation, and the individual units fell under other commands.

Tactical tail codes

During the Russian campaign many temporary units were formed and, after completing a particular task, disbanded. This flexible use of aircraft created problems with identification, assignments and organisation of the individual aircraft used in these temporary units because they were gathered from several different units, including schools.

Therefore, *Leutnant* Wasserkampf, Technical Officer of the Transport *Einsatzgruppe* 'Kupschus', invented a special tactical code system to solve this problem. A three-character code was painted on both sides of the aircraft rudder and identified the (temporary) parent unit, *Staffel* and individual aircraft. An example of this tactical code is 'B3A', found on a Ju 52/3m stationed on Crete in January 1942. The 'B' indicates that the aircraft was assigned to KGrzbV 500, commanded by *Major* Beckmann; number '3' relate to the third *Staffel*; and 'A' indicates that it belonged to the commander of that *Staffel*. (Example taken from Rosch, page 106. See also page 10 and 72 in this book for other examples.) This identification system peaked at the end of 1942 and in the beginning of 1943.

The post-war years

After the war some Ju 52s were re-assembled using spare parts at Horten Flyfabrik in Norway. The French Amiot plant at Colombes produced 415 AAC.1 'Toucan' (Ju 52/3m), which served in the Indo-China conflict and in North Africa. After these aircraft left French service in the early 1960s, the Portuguese Air Force took over some of them and kept them in flying condition until 1971.

The Spanish CASA-factory manufactured 170 CASA 352 and 352L (Ju 52/3m), which served until 1971. Various Ju 52/3m can be seen in museums worldwide, and some of them are still flying (with Deutsche Lufthansa and South African Airways, Classic Air).

Bibliography

Kössler, Karl, *Transporter – wer kennt sie schon?* Alba–Buchverlag, 1976

Piekalkiewicz, Janusz, *Die Ju 52 im Zweiten Weltkrieg.* Stuttgart: Motorbuch Verlag, 1976.

Donald, David (ed.), *Warplanes of the Luftwaffe.* Aerospace Publishing, 1994.

Feist, Uwe, and Dario, Mike, *Junkers Ju 52 in Action.* Squadron/Signal Publications, 1973.

Ketley, Barry, and Rolfe, Mark, *Luftwaffe Emblems 1939-1945.* Hikoki Publications, 1998.

Griehl, Manfred, *Ju 52 – The Luftwaffe Profile Series.* Schiffer Military.

Rosch, Barry, *Luftwaffe Codes, Markings and Units 1939-1945.* Schiffer Military, 1995.

Nowarra, Heinz J., *Die Deutsche Luftrüstung 1933-1945.* Bernhard & Graefe, 1993.

Demps and Paeschke, *Flughafen Tempelhof.* Ullstein, 1998.

Gahm, Renè, *Infantrie-Munition.* Hausen, 1998.

Cohausz, Peter W., *Deutsche Oldtimer Flugzeuge.* Aviatic Verlag, 1991.

Nelsen, Gerald, *Flugzeuge.* Stedtfeld Verlag, 1993.

Schneider, Helmut, *Flugzeugtypenbuch 1939/40.* Herm. Beyer Verlag, 1940.

Schneider, Helmut, *Flugzeugtypenbuch 1944.* Herm. Beyer Verlag, 1944.

Hildebrand, Karl F., *Die Generale Der Deutschen Luftwaffe 1933-1945, Band 3.* Biblio Verlag, 1996.

Above: The fuselage band on this Ju 52 appears to be white, indicating that the aircraft operated in the Mediterranean. Unfortunately there are no other clues to identify to which unit this aircraft belonged or what sub-type it could have been.

Below: A fleet of Ju 52s on their way to Crete in the early morning hours of 20 May 1941. At 4:30 the first Ju 52 took off and within an hour the first and second waves of the attack were on their way to Crete, as seen here. (C. König)

Left and opposite page, bottom: These Ju 52s are photographed somewhere in 1942 or 1943, whilst the tactical codes were used by the *Transportverbände* in the east and the south. One source states that this is Maleme airfield on Crete just after the airborne invasion of Crete. However, the tactical tail codes were not used at that time. The white fuselage bands indicate that the aircraft operated in the Mediterranean and it is likely that these are in North Africa or southern Italy, preparing to supply German forces in North Africa.

Below: This line of Ju 52s is probably on Maleme airfield on Crete just after the airborne invasion. All the aircraft have yellow undercowlings, a common marking for fast identification. Yellow wing tips were also used.

Left: An aircraft belonging to KGzbV 1, as indicated by the fuselage code 1Z, has just arrived in North Africa with a load of cargo. The white fuselage band indicates that the aircraft operated in the Mediterranean.

Above: This photo shows an Italian-built Savoia SM 82 flying supplies to German troops in the North African desert. The aircraft were operated by Stab III./KGzbV 1 as 5. *Staffel* in the *Gruppe*, also known as the *Savoia-Staffel* because the unit used the Savoia S.82 aircraft exclusively, unlike the rest of the *Gruppe*, which flew Ju 52s. The unit was formed in Italy in February 1942 and re-designated *Transportstaffel* 4 in May 1943.

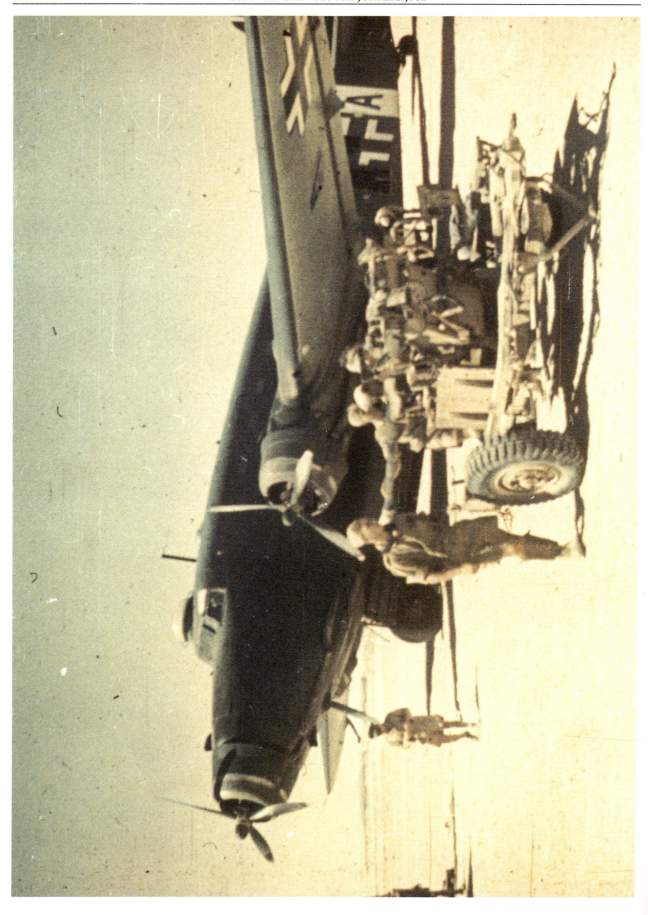

Opposite page: This Savoia SM 82 of III./KGzbV 1 has just landed and unloaded a Flak 36/37 gun in North Africa. Although considerable effort was put into supplying the *Afrikakorps* by air, it was not enough to meet the demands for food, ammunition, fuel and personnel.

Below: This Ju 52 is about to take off from a dusty forward airfield in Russia. One of the difficulties with the forward airfields was that the dirt airstrip threw up a lot of dust during take-offs and made it dangerous for other aircraft to both take off and land.

This Ju 52 of I./KGzbV 172 is photographed somewhere in the Mediterranean during 1942 or 1943, most likely Italy or North Africa. The upper fuselage cargo door is open for the loading or unloading of heavy cargo items. Note the yellow undercowlings on all engines. (Petrick)

Above: This pre-war photograph shows a Ju 52 probably at the Dessau factory, which manufactured Junkers aircraft. Although the aircraft is not finished, it has already been painted in Lufthansa colours. The wheel fairings also indicate that it was to be used by Lufthansa..

Below: In 1934 the Junkers Company sold these three Ju 52s to South Africa. Here they are seen over Germany heading south towards their destination. The three aircraft took off from Dessau on 29 October 1934 and were piloted by two German pilots, Polte and Neuenhofen, and by a South African pilot, Captain Fry.

Opposite page, top: These three Ju 52s were flown by Lufthansa before the war and were probably some of the many Ju 52s handed over to the Luftwaffe at Berlin-Tempelhof on 26 August 1939, when KGzbV 172 was formed with Lufthansa aircraft. During World War II Lufthansa continued its business on domestic and some international flights, in occupied countries.

Opposite page, bottom: This Ju 52 is being transported by road to the nearest workshop for assembling. The picture was taken in Spain in 1937 or 1938, during the Spanish Civil War. The black circle indicates that the aircraft served with the Legion Condor.

Above and below: This Ju 52 wears the civil marking, D-APYX. There is some uncertainty as to where this aircraft is photographed and what unit it belonged to. One account states that D-APYX is Ju 52/3m W.Nr. 5055; this aircraft belonged to Flugkdo. Berlin in May 1936 when the aircraft was reported at the ATG factory for overhaul. The next entry is 24 May 1941, when W.Nr. 5055 was reported by I./LLG 1 as 60 per cent damaged at Malemes airfield on Crete, due to enemy fire. The aircraft appears again in August 1942, with KGrzbV. 400 marked with unit code H4+AA and tactical code P2D. The aircraft was 80 per cent damaged near Tobruk due to engine problems. Another account states that it is being dismantled after an emergency landing near the Eastern front in 1941, which is unlikely because no aircraft bore civil markings in this format after mid-1939.

Opposite page, top: A Red Cross Ju 52, probably belonging to Sanitäts.Flugber. 3 (*Sanitätsflugbereitschaft*: Air Ambulance Duty), pictured at Rhein-Main airport in Germany. The arrangement of the people in the photo suggests a class of medical helpers who are being educated in the loading and unloading of wounded soldiers. Sanitäts.Flugber. 3 was formed in July 1941 and operated from 1941 to 1944 in the southern sector of the Eastern front.

Opposite page, bottom: These two Ju 52s are being transported along the Weser River from Weser Flugzeubau's factory at Einswarden to their Lemwerder airfield. The people passing the barge in the foreground are probably sailors as they seem to be in uniform and saluting the barge.

Above: This pre-war Ju 52 crash-landed when its left landing gear collapsed. The camouflage scheme is typical for the pre-war period, but at the beginning of the war the upper-standard Ju 52 camouflage scheme was changed to RLM 70 (Schwarzgrün – black-green) and RLM 71 (Dunkelgrün – dark green). Note the direction-finding loop that has been covered just behind the cockpit.

Below: These Ju 52s are probably parked at an Austrian airfield, March 1938. They have white numbers on the side of the engine cowling, which are some kind of non-standard marking probably applied just for one specific operation. These non-standard markings were probably removed when the operation was completed.

Above: The unit in which this Ju 52 operated with is unknown, but the small standard above the cockpit indicates that the aircraft belonged to a *Feldmarschälle* or other high-ranking officer. The wheel fairings identify it as a former Lufthansa aircraft taken over by the Luftwaffe.

Below: This Ju 52 is seen at a primitive Polish airfield where mechanics are repairing the engine in a rather hazardous way. Few Ju 52s were deployed during the Polish campaign, mainly because of the short duration of the invasion.

Above: During the Polish Campaign in September 1939 a number of Ju 52s were converted into ambulance planes in order to speed up the transport of the seriously wounded away from the front. In the beginning they were painted white all over, but later they had only a Red Cross marking applied over the *Balkenkreuz*. In January 1939 the coding system for all second-line military aircraft was changed from the standard civil registration system. The civil system had a 'D' to the left of the *Balkenkreuz*, which was replaced with 'WL' for *Wehrmacht Luft*. The marking 'WM' also appeared on aircraft, indicating *Wehrmacht Marine*.

Below: Shortly before the invasion of Norway and Denmark, this picture was taken at Neumünster airfield 31 miles (50 km) north of Hamburg. Sitting in front of the Ju 52 are some of the flying personnel of KGzbV 102, which took part in the invasion. There is an extra machine-gun position above the cockpit.

Above and below: Before operations involving a large number of Ju 52 aircraft, the airfields near the area of operation were packed tightly. The aircraft on these photographs most likely show Ju 52s belonging to the first and second Gruppe of KG2bV 1 sometime during summer or autumn, 1940. Almost all the aircraft wear a bright yellow nose band on which the unit insignia is painted.

Above: This photograph of a Ju 52, belonging to KGrzbV 102, was taken on 14 or 15 April 1940 after the aircraft had landed on Lake Hartvikvann near Narvik, Norway, on 13 April. On this aircraft were *Staffelkapitän Oblt.* Bradel, *Flugzeugführer* Fw. Böhnert, *Bordfunker Ofw.* Wilschewski, and *Bordmechaniker* Fw. Kube. This aircraft was abandoned and during the spring when the ice melted it broke through the ice and sank to the bottom of the lake. In June/August 1986 some of the 13 Ju 52s landing on the lake were raised by the *Interessengemeinschaft* Ju 52 e.V. and restored. Today one of them is on display in the Ju 52 Museum at the Wunstorf airfield near Hanover. (Wilschewski via Jessen)

Below: This Ju 52 was one of the 11 Ju 52s that landed on Lake Hartvikvann near Narvik on 13 April 1940. The aileron on the ice below the right wing was used to replace the damaged one on Ju 52 'SE+KC', W.Nr. 6664, which was the only plane to leave the lake. The aircrews of these aircraft were transported disguised as seamen and taken by train through Sweden. On the journey the windows of the train cars were painted over so that the Germans could not see through them, so they tried to scrape off some of the paint with razor blades to peek out. After the train ride the 'seamen' were transferred to the ship *Der Deutsche* and taken back to Germany. (Wilschewski via Jessen)

Above: One of the many crash-landed Ju 52s during the invasion of Norway in April 1940. These Junkers probably belong to KGrzbV 108 seen at Fornebu airfield, near Oslo. KGrzbV 108 and its Ju 52s participated in operation '*Weserübung*', and was the only *Gruppe* to remain in Norway. In May 1943 the unit was redesignated *Transportgruppe* 20.

The entire front of the aircraft has been smashed upwards in the crash.

Below: This Ju 52 (W.Nr. 5489), named 'Falken' (The Falcon), was Norwegian-operated before the war. It was taken over by the Germans after the invasion and sent to Norderney to be equipped with German radio and standard equipment. Subsequently it was handed over to Lufthansa and used for its domestic flights in Norway between Trondheim and Kirkenes. On 8 May 1945 the aircraft was taken over by *Seetransport-fliegerstaffel* 2 and flown from Hommelvik near Vêrnes to Fornbu airfield, Oslo. The aircraft was seized by the Norwegian Air Force on 27 May 1945 and painted with British roundels. It was flown by No. 21 Transport Flight based at Tromsø-Skattøra from 15 August 1945 until it was grounded 12 September 1945 and flown to Horten for overhaul for future civilian use.

Above: Paratroops jumping from a Ju 52/3m g4e, which belonged to the *Luftlandeschule* at Stendal airfield, about 62 miles (100 km) west of Berlin. Stendal served as one of the training areas for German airborne units before and during the war. (C. König)

Below: Airborne troops have just landed in a field during an exercise. In the foreground one of the airborne troops' heaviest weapons, a MG 34 on a tripod, can be seen covering incoming paratroopers. They wear the uniform of paratroopers, which was renamed *Knochensack* (sack of bones) by the soldiers. (C. König)

Above: These Ju 52s belonging to KGzbV 1 are flying over Rotterdam, probably on 10 May 1940. The Luftwaffe sustained heavy loses on 10 May with no less than 157 Ju 52s being damaged or destroyed on the ground and in the air by Dutch and British fighters.

Below: These Ju 52s are shown landing troops at Waalhaven airfield early in the morning 10 May 1940 as part of the invasion of Holland, which lasted until the surrender at 11:45 on 15 May 1940. In the background a Ju 52 is seen over Rotterdam harbour.

Opposite page: On the morning of 10 May 1940, Dutch artillery hit Rotterdam's Waalhaven airfield, which was captured by the Germans and used to fly in troops for the occupation of Holland. The bombardment hit several Ju 52s, which were damaged beyond repair, and made use of the airfield very dangerous.

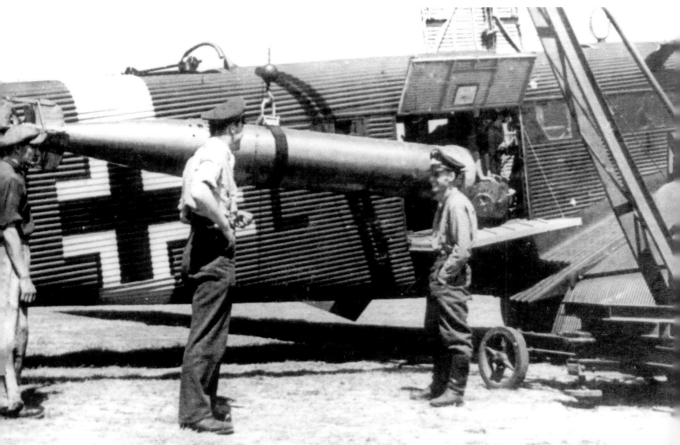

Opposite page, top: A Ju 52 photographed at Fürstenwalde airfield situated 30 km east of Berlin, 25 May 1940. The aircraft fuselage code is BB+RY indicating that it belongs to KGrzbV 105. The aircraft has a three-colour splinter camouflage scheme. (B. Rosch)

Opposite page, bottom: A torpedo is being loaded or unloaded from this Ju 52 photographed in Finland. The photograph illustrates how well the aircraft coped with big and bulky items. (Petrick)

Above: The body of *Staffelkapitän* of 3.(F)/123, Liebe-Piderit, is being returned to Germany in the latter half of 1940 after he crashed in a French Farman sports plane near Toussus-le-Buc in France, where the unit was based. On 30 June 1940 he had flown a Dornier Do 17 P-1 during a four-plane reconnaissance mission to Guernsey in the Channel Islands. Liebe-Piderit observed that the airfield on the island was unoccupied and landed. He became the first German to set foot on Guernsey prior to the planned invasion. However, when three Blenheims appeared and attacked the other Do 17s that were flying over the airfield, *Hptm.* Liebe-Piderit had to race for his aircraft and was able to return safely to base.

Below: A Ju 52 of KGzbV 2 with a line of Henschel Hs 126s and a single Fieseler Fi 156 'Storch'. The photo was probably taken in France during 1940. KGzbV 2 was never a permanent full-strength transport unit except for its *Stab*, but functioned as an umbrella organisation with various *Gruppen* when a large integrated unit was needed. It was not until May 1943 that KGzbV 2 became TG 4 and was established as a full-sized *Transportgeschwader*.

Above: A Ju 52 belonging to 1./KGrzbV 104 photographed at FFS C 11 Zeltweg in Austria, January 1941. FFS is an abbreviation for *Flugzeugführer-schule* (pilot school) and C indicates that the school trained the C licence.

Left: This Ju 52 is taking off from one of the flight schools in Germany during the winter session. In order to become a transport pilot the student had to pass the basic courses at the *A/B Schule* (elementary flying school) and then move on to take a C licence, at a *C Schule*, which required approximately 50 additional hours of training. The upper wing has a large *Balkenkreuz*.

Right: The *Feldwebel* (at right) is standing under a badly iced engine. Removing the ice was impossible without special heating equipment called a *Wärmewagen* (heat wagon). The *Wärmewagen* was a heat generator with one or more rubber hoses approximately 20 cm wide. The hot air was pumped through the hoses into the engine housing that was covered and closed off by canvas covers. If not in use, the generators were often used to heat the work tents and shops. The aircraft has its recognition letters on the edge of the wing. (Kössler)

Below: This Ju 52 displays non-standard winter camouflage pattern. However it was not unusual for Ju 52 crews to paint their aircraft all over with white paint as winter camouflage. (Nowarra via Petrick)

Opposite page, top: The crewmen of this Ju 52 are having their photograph taken in Norway in April, 1940. The emblem on the side of the aircraft's nose indicates that they served with 2./KGrzbV 105. This unit was withdrawn from the country on 30 April 1940. (Junkers Werksfoto via Nowarra)

Opposite page, bottom: This close-up of a Ju 52/MS gives a good impression of how the mine ring was attached to the fuselage and wing of the aircraft. *Minensuchgruppe* 1, which this aircraft probably belonged, was divided in six *Staffeln* that each had a geographical area that they operated in. (M. Griehl)

Above: The full size of the mine ring can be seen from below. The mine ring was constructed by 44-in (14-mm) aluminium rods forming a coil encapsulated in an aluminium casing. Aluminium was used instead of copper because copper is approximately three times heavier, however not three times as good an electrical conductor. (M. Griehl)

Below: These two Ju 52/MS aircraft are seen flying low over the water at the entrance to a harbour. They are in the process of clearing the harbour area. The magnetic field was only effective in shallow waters such as harbours, rivers, and coast areas. (M. Griehl)

Above: A Ju 52 equipped with mine ring at Semlin airbase in Yugoslavia 1941. The minesweeper version of the Ju 52 was nicknamed 'Mausi' and the ring measured 49 ft (14-15m) in diameter. The ring was a magnetic generator which caused detonation of specific types of sea mines when flying low over them. The mines were designed to explode when a metal ship passed over, but instead the magnetic field triggered the mines.

Below: These two Ju 52/3m g4e belong to I./KGzbV 1 and are being serviced on a dusty airfield somewhere in Greece during spring 1941. The yellow rudders and engine cowlings indicate Greece during the Crete operation. KGzbV 1 was formed on 26 August 1939 in Gardelegen from KGrzbV 1. (C. König)

Opposite page, top: This Ju 52 of 13./KGzbV 1 hit a ditch at the end of the landing strip while bringing supplies to 4./JG 27 in the Balkans in 1941. The undercarriage was more liable to collapse when the aircraft was loaded with supplies if obstacles were encountered on the airfield.

Opposite page, bottom: An aircraft of KGzbV 2 is being loaded with troops for the airborne invasion of Crete on 20 May 1941. There is a wavy metal bar for the hand-held machine gun in the centre window. It was made to prevent the gunner from shooting up his own wing or engine.

Above: The first Ju 52 took off at 4:30, and within an hour the first and second wave of attack were en route to Crete. The first wave consisted of towed gliders; the second wave of Ju 52s was loaded with *Fallschirmjäger*. The airborne units used for the invasion of Crete were the *Fallschirmjäger-Regiment* 1, 2 and 3 (FJR 1) under 1. *Fallschirm-Jäger-Division*. On paper, a regiment (3,206 men) consisted of 3 battalions (I, II and III), each with four companies (1-4, 5-8, 9-12), a 13th company (Anti-tank), and a 14th company (Mortar).

Below: A Ju 52 towing a DFS 230 assault glider. The DFS 230 was used to transport troops to be landed behind enemy lines. The DFS 230 could carry nine fully armed combat troops and a pilot with a maximum weight of 4,620 lb (2,100 kg). In all 2230 DFS 230 gliders were built, and it became the standard assault transport glider in the Luftwaffe.

Opposite page: The Ju 52 tow plane can be seen from the cockpit of a DFS 230 glider plane. The DFS 230 glider was used in operations for the first time during the capture of the Belgian fort at Eben Emael and also extensively during the airborne invasion of Crete, where 80 of these gliders participated.

Left: These two Ju 52s crash-landed on the beach near Maleme airfield on Crete, 20 May 1941 while transporting mountain troops, which were to be deployed in support of the fighting units trying to overcome the last pockets of British resistance. Crete was not in German hands before the British evacuated the island during the night of 31 May/1 June 1941.

Below: A new *Gruppenkommandeure* speaks to his unit in Italy before taking over its operations. The covers on the engines and cockpit protected mechanical parts from rough weather.

Opposite page, top: Unloading supplies for 4./JG 27 in 1941. The pilots and ground personnel are probably being given mail from Germany, as they do not look like they are actively participating in the unloading.

Opposite page, bottom: This photograph was taken in Bulgaria or Russia in 1941. To the extreme left the *Gruppenkommandeur* of II./JG 27, Hptm. Wolfgang Lippert, can be seen. There is a white fuselage band above the upper cargo door, and the electrical generator on the right side of the fuselage top has been removed.

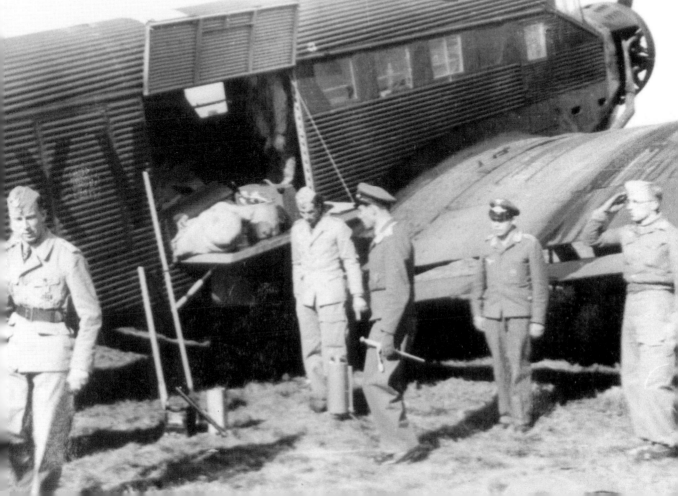

Opposite page, top: These Indian POWs are unloading supplies from a Ju 52 on an airfield near Tobruk in 1941. The aircraft belongs to KGzbV 1, which flew numerous supply missions to North Africa over the Mediterranean from Sicily and southern Italy. The Indian POWs are soldiers from some of the Indian units that fought under British command in North Africa.

Opposite page, bottom: A Ju 52 operating with KGzbV 1 in North Africa, probably just after landing. It is being unloaded so that it can take off and return to Sicily or Italy.

Above: This line of Ju 52s is pictured in Norway 1940. The stripes on the wing engine cowls indicate that the aircraft belongs to the first *Staffel* of their unit, which was either KGrzbV 101 or 108. However, this marking was not standard and only used sporadically throughout the transport units of the Luftwaffe.

Below: A 13./KGzbV 1 Ju 52 bringing supplies to Russia during the summer of 1941. At this time KGzbV 1 sub units operated in both the east and the south. The unit receiving the supplies was II./JG 27, which operated in Russia before being transferred to Ain-el-Gazala in North Africa 24 September 1941.

Left: This Ju 52 based in Russia is probably in the process of getting its bent propeller changed. The stripes on the wing were some kind of identification marking. This position for a marking was not usual, but the marking itself is unknown. The marking appears on both wings.

Above: A Ju 52 of 4./KGzbV 1 has tipped over on the icy runway at Saporosjhe airfield in Ukraine during the winter late in 1941. There are big areas of yellow on the wing tips, which was standard for many German aircraft to make recognition for friendly ground forces easier.

Opposite page, bottom: A Ju 52 belonging to I./KGzbV 1 passing over German hospital tents near Benghasi, Libya in 1942. Note the non-standard number '4' on the tail rudder, which is most likely an individual aircraft identification mark.

Below: A Ju 52 in Norway during 1941. The 7.92 mm MG 15 gun position above the cockpit was an addition made primarily to the g7e, and designated 'DL-15A Rüstsatz'. It was made when Ju 52 crews called attention to the lack of a forward defence weapon. Note the numbers below the cockpit.

Above and opposite page: Japanese Lieutenant General Ōshima Hiroshi on a visit to the Russian front in 1942. Ōshima was the Japanese ambassador in Berlin during the war and had access to a great deal of information on the German-Russian war. On several occasions Ōshima visited Hitler's headquarters in East Prussia, but he also inspected the German troops near the front and was impressed by their standards. On these photos he wears the uniform of a lieutenant general of the Imperial Japanese Army.

Below: A production line of Ju 52s at the Junkers Flugzeug- und Motorenwerke AG at Bernburg, 60 km north of Leipzig, Germany. The production of Ju 52 peaked in 1943 when 887 Ju 52 aircraft were produced at various factories.

Above: This Ju 52 was photographed at Stubendorf airfield in Oberschlesien (Upper Silesia), Germany, 1942. The fuselage identification markings on this aircraft reveals a clue as to which unit operated it, but the *Werknummer*, which is most likely 5530, identifies it as a Ju 52/3m ge. W.Nr. 5530 flew for the first time at Dessau on 12 February 1936 and was registered D-AKUV. It served with 4./KGrzbV 600 when it was hit by AA fire near Salutsche in Russia on 20 March 1942 and one crew member was wounded. Stubendorf airfield was home to *Fliegerschule A/B* 110, that was to become *Blindflugschule* 11 in 1943.

Below: These Ju 52s are on their way to the Crimea in Russia with supplies in 1942. They are accompanied by three Ju 87s

belonging to St.G. 2 (*Stukageschwader* dive bomber unit).

Opposite page, top: The same aircraft as below is pictured during 1942 or 1943, just after arriving at an airfield in North Africa with a load of fuel barrels and supplies. The emblem, which is most likely yellow, judging by the contrast to the 'K' on the edge of the wing, indicates that the aircraft belongs to 11./KGzbV 1.

Opposite page, bottom: An aircraft of III./KGzbV 1 on its way over the Mediterranean to or from North Africa. The yellow 'K' on the edge of the wing designates it as a particular aircraft within 11. *Staffel*. Markings of this type were not standard, but were not uncommon.

Opposite page, top: This Ju 52/3m belonging to 1./KGrzbV 105 is flying supplies to the Russian front. Both the fuselage code (G6+EX) and the emblem, which consists of an oil barrel with wings, indicate KGrzbV 105. The first *Staffel* of KGrzbV 105 was formed during April 1940 in Kiel. The aircraft has unevenly distributed remaining white winter camouflage.

Opposite page, bottom: During a landing on a muddy airfield in Russia, this Ju 52 of 2./KGzbV 106, piloted by Uffz. Hans Hellhake, bent one of its propeller blades. It has a number '2' on the front engine and a single red stripe on the left engine indicating 2. *Staffel.* (Kössler)

Above: A fleet of Ju 52s passes low over a small Russian village in the vicinity of Sŭkŭnikowo. The aircraft do not appear to have a fighter escort, so they could be flying at a safe distance from the front or flying low to avoid detection by Soviet fighters.

Below: This Ju 52 seen in Russia during the winter of 1943/44 belongs to III./TG 3 (former KGzbV 102). The aircraft is most likely dark green (RLM 71) as there is little contrast with the *Balkenkreuz* – a colour commonly used on school aircraft.

Above: This former 5./KGzbV 1 aircraft was fitted with floats and deployed with LTStaffel (See) 1 (*Lufttransport-staffel:* Air Transport Unit). The aircraft is taking off from the Aegean Sea off the coast of Greece. The camouflage is unusual for a seaplane; usually only land-based aircraft were painted with the white winter camouflage.

Below: On the Russian front a Ju 52 of IV./KGzbV 1 is having its white winter camouflage colour scheme re-applied with broomsticks during the winter of 1942/43. The fuselage code 1Z has been painted over, along with some of the cabin windows.

Opposite page, top: This Ju 52 was a total write-off after a landing accident in the winter of 1942/43 on a snow-covered runway at Gardermoen airfield, just north of Oslo. It was the major airfield in the area during the war. The Germans also heavily expanded it during the years when Norway was occupied.

Opposite page, bottom: A Ju 52 photographed in Russia during wintertime. Although this Ju 52 features an extra large cargo door, the task of loading and unloading of bulky cargo without a truck or other machinery was often difficult.

Above: A Ju 52 belonging to II./KGzbV 1, in Russia during 1942 or 1943. The emblem is a combination of the previous emblem: a Brandenburg eagle carrying a sword in its claws, and a shield with an Austrian double-headed eagle (there is also a marking near the wing). It was introduced by *Major* Neundlinger in mid-1941. Although the photograph does not show a gun installation above the cockpit, the aircraft seems to have an opening as the crew member is sitting with his legs halfway into the cockpit.

Opposite page, top: After the winter was over the water-based paint used for winter camouflage had to be removed. This Ju 52 operated with an unknown unit at Bagerowo airfield in the Crimea early in 1943.

Opposite page, bottom: A Ju 52 of an unknown unit based at Bagerowo airfield in the Crimea early in 1943. The unit's mission at this time was to re-supply the army units fighting on the Caucasus front after the battle for Stalingrad.

Above: This photograph was taken in March 1943 at Bari airfield in Italy, which served as a staging field for Africa. The Ju 52 in the foreground was formerly a LLG 1 aircraft (*Luftlandegeschwader*: Air Landing Unit), but in May 1943 it belonged to KGrzbV 5. The Ju 52s are sharing the airfield with 7. and 9. *Staffel* of JG 27, which were based there for a short time in May 1943 before moving to Trapani later that month.

Below: The wing of this Ju 52 was damaged by Russian flak over the Kuban battle sector in the southern area of the front during the summer months of 1943. The aircraft belonged to III./TG 3, which supplied the isolated German-Romanian 17th Army in the Kuban steppes, north of the Caucasus.

Above: This Ju 52 is coded G6+LX and belonged to 1./KGrzbV 105. The aircraft is photographed dropping supplies over the Russian farmland, probably during early springtime, as most of the winter camouflage is still visible. A crew member is manning the fuselage gun position. (B. Rosch)

Right: This Ju 52 of an unknown unit is seen during a primitive repair at the Bagerowo airfield in the Crimea during 1943. The left tyre is flat and has to be changed, so the men are standing on the wing for counter-weight.

Opposite page, top: An anti-aircraft position high above an airfield. The gun is a ¾-in (2cm) Flak 38, which was commonly used in air defence of airfields. The photograph shows many different types of aircraft on the airfield: a dozen Ju 52s, two Ju 88, two Bf 109, two Bf 110, one Fw 190, one Fw 200 and two liaison aircraft.

Opposite page, bottom: Two Ju 52s belonging to 2./KGzbV 1 flying over Tunisian landscape in early 1943. The 1Z fuselage code indicates that the unit of the aircraft is KGzbV 1 and the barely visible red K designates that it belongs to the second *Staffel*. The usual window/gun position is in the upper cargo door in the fuselage. (B. Rosch)

Top: These aircraft of I./KGzbV 1 are shown taking off from the Catania airfield on Sicily probably during April 1943, when the Luftwaffe tried to evacuate the German troops in Tunisia. This operation took its toll on the *Transportverbände* when they lost 432 transport aircraft, almost all of which were Ju 52/3m.

Below: A bomb hit this Ju 52 during an air raid in spring 1943. It was supplying the German troops in Tunisia by air because the Mediterranean had become very dangerous for supply vessels. During 1943 hardly any of the ships that sailed off from Italy or Greece reached their ports in North Africa unscratched.

Above: This Ju 52 belonging to 2./KGrzbV 105 is pictured after a landing accident at Heiligenbeil airfield, East Prussia, in 1943. The unit emblem painted on the nose is an oil barrel with wings, which can be found in different variations depending upon the particular *Staffel* of KGrzbV 105.

Below: Paratroopers are loading their equipment onto a Ju 52 in the Crimea during 1942 or 1943. The aircraft belongs to LLG 1 (*Luftlandegeschwader*. Air Landing Unit), which assisted the fighting in the Crimea. LLG 1 was formed 27

July 1940 in Hildesheim and operated on most of the fighting fronts during the war.

Opposite page, top and bottom: The undercarriage of this Ju 52 broke whilst landing on a muddy airstrip in Russia. The skull and bones emblem are painted on both sides of the nose. It isn't clear as to which unit the aircraft belonged; one account states 1./TG1, but this isn't verified.

Opposite page, top:
Close-up of an anti-tank weapon mounted between the wheels of a Ju 52 for transportation. The weapon is probably a 10.5 cm *Leichtgeschutz* that fired a fixed-charge rocket shell. Several different objects could be mounted, such as motorcycles, bigger machine guns and cannons. These objects were sometimes fitted with parachutes or packed in jettison-capable frames with shock absorbers. (C. König)

Opposite page, bottom: The emblem on the nose on this Ju 52, belonging to 2./KGrzbV 9, shows '*Auntie* Ju' carrying two luggage bags. '*Auntie* Ju' was one of the popular nicknames given to the Ju 52 by many German pilots.

Right: The title of this photograph reads 'Last snack before flight over the Black Sea, Caucasus'. It gives a good impression of the uniform and equipment that German flyers had to wear when going on a mission.

Left: Wounded soldiers from the Eastern front being helped aboard a Ju 52 from TG 3 during 1943 or 1944. The wavy metal bar for the hand-held machine gun is on the second window from the right, intended to prevent the gunner from shooting up his own wing or engine.

Opposite page, bottom: A Ju 52 having its wheels dug free before taking off from an airfield on the Eastern front. The two cylindrical devices under and behind each engine are oil coolers. Each engine had its own separate oil-cooling system.

Above: A Ju 52/3m g7e and the two Ju 52s in the background belong to 4./TG 1 and are pictured at Pütnitz/Pommern in Germany, April 1945. Only the 4th *Staffel* of TG 1 operated aircraft with floats.

Below: The same aircraft as bottom left is being fuelled. The two over-painted yellow stripes around the fuselage indicate that the aircraft was flown earlier in its career by a *Blindflugschule*.

Above: Ju 52s of TG 1 on an airfield on the Russian front during 1943 or 1944. The photo shows some of the primitive conditions under which the Luftwaffe had to operate.

Below: This is Ju 252 V5, marked DF + BQ (later J4 + LH), being made ready for flight in 1943. The aircraft served with LTS 290 (*Lufttransportstaffel* 290) until it was destroyed at Grosseto airfield, Italy, in May 1943. The unit, also known as *Viermotorigetransportsstaffel*, flew the four-engine Ju 290. The prototypes V5 to V15 were all designated A-1 and put into service in the second half of 1942. Other Ju 252s were issued by *Gruppe* 'Gartenfeldt', whose primary task was to drop agents in North Africa for the *Reichssicherheitshauptamt* (National security headquarters).

Above: This Ju 52 belonged to *Luftverkehrsgruppe* 'Rangsdorf', as indicated by the A7+HL marking on the fuselage. It was found by the Allies near Mons, Belgium in the second half of 1944. *Luftverkehrsgruppe* Rangsdorf consisted of an A, B and C *Staffel* that were all formed in May 1944. The unit existed for only a few months before it was disbanded in October 1944.

Below: This Romanian Ju 52 was at Popestii Airport in Bucharest at the time American POWs were rescued by American forces and flown to Italy. The rescue operation took place in the first week of September, 1944. Some Soviet aircraft were also on the base while this rescue operation was carried out.

Above: *Feltmarschall* Hugo Sperrle visits IV./KG 26 at Toulouse/Francasal airfield in the Midi-Pyrenees region of south-western France, in 1944. For a shorter period of time this unit trained Spanish crews on the Ju 88, which was the unit's primary aircraft.

Below: A Ju 52/3m g5e, W.Nr. 7279, coded 4V+BP. This aircraft belonged to III./TG 2 and was one of two that force-landed on 22 January 1945 south-west of Asselborn, in Luxembourg, after being damaged by enemy fire. It is fitted with flame dampers for night operations. The aircraft were most likely supplying army units withdrawing from the area after the failed offensive in the Ardennes. Note the big yellow outer part of the wing, which wasa commanly used identification marking for German aircraft.

Above: These Ju 52s are most likely somewhere in northern Italy, Yugoslavia or Greece. The only clue to their identity is the seemingly white fuselage band on the second aircraft from the right, used on aircraft operating in the Mediterranean theatre.

Below: This aircraft is reputedly Hermann Göring's personal aircraft. The aircraft is pictured on an airfield near Salzburg, Austria in 1945 after the German surrender. In the background is a Fieseler Fi 156 'Storch' with either a customary *Balkenkreuz* or a Red Cross marking on the fuselage.

Left: A crew serving with I./TG 1 in front of their Ju 52 a few days after the surrender in May 1945. Second from the left is the pilot, *Oberfeldwebel* Siegfried Godau. They are pictured near Niebüll, close to the Danish border, just before blowing up the aircraft to prevent it falling into enemy hands.

Bottom left: The same aircraft as above, burning in a field just outside Niebüll. According to a German statement to 2. Tactical Air Force RAF 5 May 1945, I./TG 1 was based at Westerland, Germany on the island of Sylt close to the Danish border. The unit was equipped with 14 Ju 52 land aircraft and 11 Ju 52 sea aircraft, and consisted of 248 men.

Opposite page, top: After the war the RAF used this Ju 352 A-1 for evaluation purposes. It is seen in southern Germany, 1945, before being ferried to England. Only 46 Ju 352 A-1s were produced before the programme was cancelled due to the course of the war. At least two Ju 352 A-1s survived, one going to the RAF and the other finding its way to Czechoslovakia.

Opposite page, bottom: The Ju 52 was used in Portugal during the post-war years until the early 1960s, as both personnel and cargo transport. This photograph was taken in Gibraltar. All military equipment (direction-finding loop and gun) has been removed and two roof windows have been installed instead.

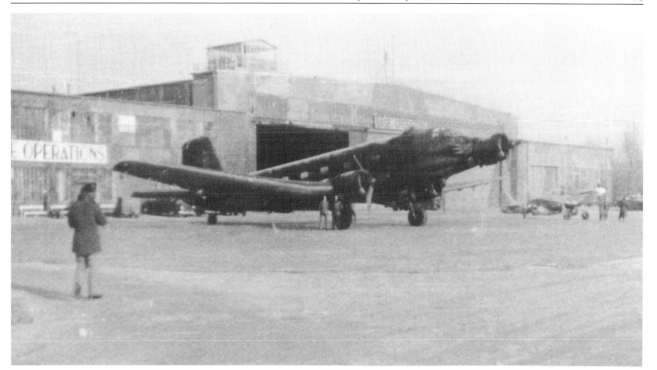

Above: This photograph shows, in detail, the corrugated duralumin skinning on the Ju 52. By the end of the war this aircraft was found at Landshut airfield in Bavaria, approximately 43 miles (70 km) northeast of Munich. The aircraft belonged to 7./TG 2 former 2./KGrzbV 800.

Below: This Ju 52 was piled up at München/Riem airfield 4–5 miles (6–8 km) east of Munich in 1945, together with at least five Me 262s and several Fw 190s. The München/Riem airfield was used by JV 44, a jet fighter unit commanded by Adolf Galland.